RACE AND POLICING IN MODERN AMERICA

BY DUCHESS HARRIS, JD, PHD
WITH R. L. VAN

Core Library

Cover image: A protester faces police in Washington, DC, on
June 3, 2020. People were protesting against police brutality.

An Imprint of Abdo Publishing
abdobooks.com

JUV NONFIC 305.8 HAR

abdobooks.com

Published by Abdo Publishing, a division of ABDO, PO Box 398166, Minneapolis, Minnesota 55439.
Copyright © 2021 by Abdo Consulting Group, Inc. International copyrights reserved in all countries.
No part of this book may be reproduced in any form without written permission from the publisher.
Core Library™ is a trademark and logo of Abdo Publishing.

Printed in the United States of America, North Mankato, Minnesota
102020
012021

THIS BOOK CONTAINS
RECYCLED MATERIALS

Cover Photo: Bill Clark/CQ Roll Call/AP Images
Interior Photos: Alex Sanz/AP Images, 4–5; Jeffrey Collins/AP Images, 7; North Wind Picture
Archives, 11; Seth Wenig/AP Images, 14–15, 43; Matt Rourke/AP Images, 16; Library of Congress,
19; Red Line Editorial, 21, 26; John Nacion/STAR MAX/IPx/AP Images, 24–25; Kevork Djansezian/AP
Images, 28; Allison C. Bailey/Shutterstock Images, 32–33, 35; Don Campbell/The Herald-Palladium/
AP Images, 37; John J. Watkins/The Times/AP Images, 39

Editor: Katharine Hale
Series Designer: Sarah Taplin

Library of Congress Control Number: 2020944140

Publisher's Cataloging-in-Publication Data

Names: Harris, Duchess, author. | Van, R. L., author.
Title: Race and policing in modern America / by Duchess Harris and R. L. Van
Description: Minneapolis, Minnesota : Abdo Publishing, 2021 | Series: Core library guide to racism in
    modern America | Includes online resources and index
Identifiers: ISBN 9781532194689 (lib. bdg.) | ISBN 9781644945117 (pbk.) | ISBN 9781098214203
    (ebook)
Subjects: LCSH: Police-community relations--United States--Juvenile literature. | Police--United
    States--Juvenile literature. | Police ethics--Juvenile literature. | United States--History--Juvenile
    literature. | Race relations--Juvenile literature.
Classification: DDC 305.8--dc23

CONTENTS

FOUNDATIONS OF A FLAWED SYSTEM

I t was October 2015. Niya Kenny was in algebra class in Columbia, South Carolina. Her classmate Shakara was using her cell phone during class. The teacher called a school administrator to take Shakara out of class. But Shakara would not leave. Then, the administrator called for a school resource officer (SRO).

SROs are police officers. They work in schools. Their job is to keep students safe.

Niya and Shakara were students at Spring Valley High School in South Carolina.

Ben Fields was the school's SRO. He is white. Niya and Shakara are both Black.

Fields entered the classroom. Niya had heard that Fields was aggressive. She started taking a video on her phone. Fields asked Shakara to get up. She refused. Fields grabbed Shakara. He put his arm around her neck. Fields flipped her and her desk to the ground. Shakara fought back. He dragged her across the room. Fields injured Shakara during the incident.

Niya was shocked. She cried and yelled. She defended Shakara. She asked other people in the room if they were going to let this happen.

Fields pinned Shakara to the ground. He handcuffed her. Then he turned to Niya. Fields took Niya to jail too.

At the time, South Carolina enforced a disturbing schools law. Misbehaving or distracting others in class was a crime. A report by the American Civil Liberties Union found this law disproportionately affected

People protested the criminal charges that were filed against Niya and Shakara. Some people called for Ben Fields to be charged instead.

Black students. They were about four times more likely than white students to be charged with breaking it. The report noted the difference in discipline could not be explained by differences in student behavior depending on race. Niya and Shakara were charged under this law.

The charges were later dropped. Fields lost his job. But he was not charged with a crime. Niya did not to go back to school. She became anxious and uncomfortable around police officers. Niya talked to Shakara after the incident. She told reporters Shakara was traumatized.

Some considered this incident an example of police brutality. Police brutality is the use of excessive force by police officers. It is an important issue to address in the United States.

CRIMINAL JUSTICE IN THE UNITED STATES

Policing is part of the criminal justice system. This system has three main parts. These are law enforcement, courts, and corrections. Law enforcement workers respond to emergency calls. They investigate crimes. They also arrest suspected criminals. Police officers are law enforcement workers. Prosecutors decide whether to charge someone with a crime. Then the courts decide whether that person is guilty. If the person is guilty, courts decide the punishment. The correctional system carries out punishments. These include jail and prison sentences. The correctional system also helps people return to society after their sentences are served.

There is racial inequality in the criminal justice system. However, this inequality has roots outside the system. People living in poverty or exposed to violent crime are more likely to commit crimes. In 2019, nearly 19 percent of Black people lived in poverty. Only 7.3 percent of white people lived in poverty. In addition, 62 percent of Black people live

A RESPONSE TO POLICE BRUTALITY

In 1919 a Black boy named Eugene Williams was swimming at a lake in Chicago, Illinois. White people did not want Black people there. A group of white people attacked and killed Eugene. The police did not arrest them. Black people protested. In response, white people attacked them. Hundreds were injured. Thirty-eight people died.

A study of the incident was published in 1922. It found that police attacked and arrested the Black protesters. They ignored the crimes white people committed. The report made suggestions for how to prevent similar incidents. However, the report was mostly ignored.

in neighborhoods with high rates of violent crime. Police often overpolice these neighborhoods, arresting residents for minor crimes. But researchers say these neighborhoods are underpoliced when it comes to preventing and solving violent crime. This causes residents to feel both harassed by and abandoned by the police.

RACISM AND THE ROOTS OF POLICING

Policing in early US history was very different from today. People in the American South created slave patrols in the 1700s. These were groups of white men who enforced slave codes. Slave codes were laws that controlled enslaved people. Slave patrols arrested slaves who ran away. The patrols used violent punishments.

In 1865 the US Congress passed the Thirteenth Amendment. It made slavery illegal. But it allowed prisons to force people convicted of crimes into

The New York City Police Department, formed in 1845, is among the oldest police forces in the United States. This woodcut from the 1890s shows officers caring for an abandoned infant.

unpaid labor. Plantation owners could pay the state to use prisoners for work. Prisons also forced people to work on railroads and in mines. These jobs were often dangerous. Southern states passed new laws to control Black people. These were called Jim Crow laws. Under these laws, Black people could be sent to prison very easily. Black people also often served longer sentences than white people. Some Black prisoners did not live long enough to experience freedom again.

In the North, early police forces began to form in the 1830s. The first modern police force was created in 1838 in Boston, Massachusetts. Soon other major

THE BLACK PANTHERS

The Black Panther Party for Self-Defense (BPP) was created in California in 1966. It was a political party. The BPP's goal was to protect Black people from police brutality. BPP members carried guns and watched police interact with Black people. They reminded police of people's rights. The BPP wanted social and economic justice for Black people. It also started social programs in Black communities. These included free breakfast for kids and free health clinics.

cities established police forces. Black people and immigrants were a big part of city workforces. The police could use force to control workers who went on strike.

The civil rights era saw more instances of police brutality. In the mid-1960s, civil rights leaders led protests against this brutality. Police officers broke up protests. Some used violence. The civil rights movement led to major changes in racial equality. However, systemic racism and police brutality continue today.

STRAIGHT TO THE
SOURCE

In the 1960s, John Lewis was a civil rights activist. He later became a politician. In 1963, he addressed police brutality in a speech at the March on Washington protest in Washington, DC:

> There is nothing [in the administration's civil rights bill] to protect the young children and old women who must face police dogs and fire hoses in the South while they engage in peaceful demonstrations. . . . It will not protect the hundreds and thousands of people that have been arrested on trumped charges. . . . To those who have said, "Be patient and wait," we have long said that we cannot be patient. We do not want our freedom gradually, but we want to be free now! . . . We are tired of being beaten by policemen. We are tired of seeing our people locked up in jail over and over again.

Source: John Lewis. "Speech at the March on Washington (28 Aug. 1963)." *Voices of Democracy: The US Oratory Project*, n.d., voicesofdemocracy.umd.edu. Accessed 10 Aug. 2020.

BACK IT UP

In his speech, Lewis used evidence to support his point. Write a paragraph describing the point Lewis was making. Then write down two or three pieces of evidence he used to make that point.

SYSTEMIC RACISM

A person's skin color should not affect how he or she is treated by the criminal justice system. But many laws and policies affect people of color more than white people. People of color are often at a disadvantage. This is called systemic racism.

STOPS

Stop-and-frisk programs allow police officers to stop anyone they think looks suspicious. Police officers can search the person's belongings.

Many activists, including Reverend Al Sharpton, *center*, have protested stop-and-frisk policies. These policies disproportionately affect people of color.

Philadelphia Police Commissioner Richard Ross says stop-and-frisk programs are important to stopping gun violence. He also says poverty is the cause of gun violence, so addressing poverty would reduce the need for these programs.

The goal of stop-and-frisk programs is to prevent crime. For example, police take away illegal drugs or weapons.

New York City's stop-and-frisk program grew in the early 2000s. But police officers did not stop people equally. In 2011, 53 percent of people stopped were Black and 34 percent were Latino. Just 9 percent of people stopped were white. Out of 685,724 recorded stops, 88 percent of people were innocent. This means they were not arrested or ordered to appear in court.

In 2013 a court found New York City's stop-and-frisk policy to be unconstitutional. It said the stops were discriminatory. Stop-and-frisk programs are still allowed. But officers cannot enforce them based on what someone looks like. The number of total stops in New York City has gone down. But Black people are still targeted. In 2019, 59 percent of people stopped in New York City were Black. Again, only 9 percent were white.

PERSPECTIVES

THE RECEIVING END OF STOP AND FRISK

Studies show that police stops can cause anxiety, depression, and post-traumatic stress disorder (PTSD). In 2011 and 2012, the Center for Constitutional Rights interviewed people who had been stopped and frisked in New York City. Both years, 87 percent of people stopped were Black or Latino. People said the police engaged in violence and sexual harassment during the stops. Interviewees felt humiliated and traumatized. One said, "When they stop you in the street, and then everybody's looking . . . it does degrade you. And then people get the wrong perception of you."

Similar discrimination takes place during traffic stops. A 2016 report found that in Chicago, police stopped and searched Black and Hispanic drivers four times more often than white drivers. But white drivers were twice as likely to have illegal items. A 2015 study in Greensboro, North Carolina, found that police were more likely to use force against Black drivers. Police sometimes stopped Black drivers for no legal reason.

THE WAR ON DRUGS

Discriminatory laws affect people across the country. President Richard Nixon started a program called the War on Drugs in June 1971. It was meant to control illegal drug use in the United States. Presidents Ronald Reagan and Bill Clinton expanded this program in the 1980s and 1990s. Police received more money to enforce drug laws. New laws set strict minimum sentences for drug offenses.

The War on Drugs has had negative effects on people of color. Police search people of color at a

Richard Nixon, who began the federal War on Drugs, served as US president from 1969 to 1974.

higher rate than white people. Black people use and sell illegal drugs at approximately the same rate as white people. But they are caught with illegal drugs more often. They are also six times more likely to be put in prison for drug offenses than white people.

THE SCHOOL-TO-PRISON PIPELINE

The criminal justice system negatively affects people of color from an early age. Many schools in the United States have SROs. Schools hire SROs to protect students. But having police in schools can have harmful effects. Students in schools with police may be arrested instead of being disciplined by the school. Students then enter the criminal justice system. This puts them at greater risk for dropping out of school. Students who leave school are less likely to find work. They are more likely to turn to crime. This becomes a pattern. Critics call this pattern the school-to-prison pipeline. Black students receive harsher punishments than white students for breaking similar rules. They are expelled at three times the rate of white students. Black students are also three times more likely to be arrested. Students of color are more likely to attend schools with a police officer on-site.

EFFECTS ON SOCIETY

The United States has the highest number of people in prison in the world. In 2018, 2.1 million people were in prison or jail. That year Black people made up 32.9 percent of federal and state prisoners. But only about 12 percent of the US population was Black.

THE SCHOOL-TO-PRISON
PIPELINE

This graph shows the rates of preschool suspensions and the rates of student arrests for both Black and white students for the 2015–2016 school year. What do you notice about these numbers? How does the information shown in the graph help you understand the school-to-prison pipeline?

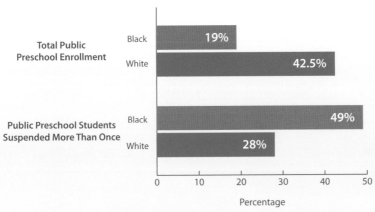

Preschool Enrollment and Suspensions

Total Public Preschool Enrollment — Black 19% | White 42.5%

Public Preschool Students Suspended More Than Once — Black 49% | White 28%

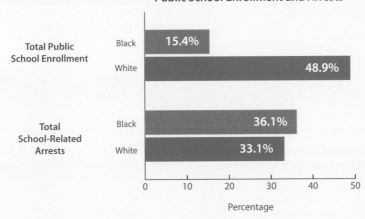

Public School Enrollment and Arrests

Total Public School Enrollment — Black 15.4% | White 48.9%

Total School-Related Arrests — Black 36.1% | White 33.1%

People who are in prison lose many rights. Prisoners can be forced to work. They are paid very little, if at all. They often lose the right to vote. In 48 states, felons cannot vote while they are in the criminal justice system. In some cases, felons can lose voting rights even after being released from prison. The felon population is disproportionately Black. This means Black people are denied the right to vote at a much higher rate than white people. In 2016 one in every 13 Black American adults did not have the right to vote. This was a total of 2.2 million people.

STRAIGHT TO THE
SOURCE

Keisha Blain is an associate professor of history at the University of Pittsburgh. In an interview with NPR, she spoke about the history of race and policing in the United States:

> *I think the fundamental problem is structural racism. And this is something that we have not actually dealt with. And so we keep having conversations about how we might tweak this or tweak that. Maybe we'll pass some policy that's anti–choke hold, and that sounds wonderful. But if you don't actually get to the root of the problem, then you'll find yourself in the same place over and over again, even if you pass a hundred different policies that say, don't choke a person; don't place your knee on a person's neck. . . . In the end, the system has to be radically changed.*

> Source: "The History of Policing and Race in the US Are Deeply Intertwined." *All Things Considered from NPR*, 13 June 2020, npr.org. Accessed 10 Aug. 2020.

CONSIDER YOUR AUDIENCE

Adapt this passage for a different audience, such as your principal or friends. Write a blog post conveying this same information for the new audience. How does your post differ from the original text and why?

USE OF FORCE AND JUSTICE

It can be hard to tell when an officer's use of force becomes excessive. Police may use force while arresting people. Police sometimes kill people during these arrests. The use of force in these cases is often found to be legal and justified. Police have to make split-second decisions in dangerous situations. Sometimes officers need to use force to keep themselves safe. But some people believe that police can use too much force. They say police sometimes use force in situations

Police officers are often in dangerous situations where they have to make quick decisions. But some people think police respond with violence too often.

PUBLIC VIEWS OF THE POLICE

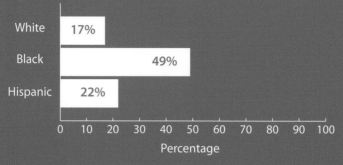

**Percentage of Americans Who Feel Less
Secure When They See a Police Officer**

White	17%
Black	49%
Hispanic	22%

Percentage
(0 10 20 30 40 50 60 70 80 90 100)

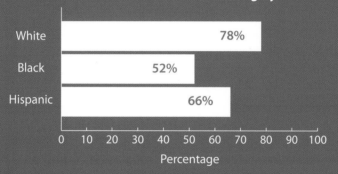

**Percentage of Americans Who Would Rate
Police Officers' Ethics Highly**

White	78%
Black	52%
Hispanic	66%

Percentage
(0 10 20 30 40 50 60 70 80 90 100)

The charts above show some views that Americans have of
police and their ethics. *Ethics* means guidelines and beliefs
about what is right and wrong. What do you notice about these
numbers? How do these charts convey information differently
from the text of Chapter Three? How does the information
in Chapter Three help you understand the information in
these charts?

where violence could be prevented. Police use force

on Black people almost four times as often as they do

on white people. An analysis from the *Guardian* found

that Black people killed by police were twice as likely to be unarmed when compared to white people killed by police. FBI data shows that Black people make up a disproportionate number of those killed when not attacking.

CRIES FOR JUSTICE

People have been protesting police brutality for decades. One incident happened in 1991. A Black man named Rodney King led police on a car chase. When officers reached King, they wanted to stop him from getting away. Some officers beat him with their batons. Others stood by and watched. The beating caused King permanent brain damage and other injuries. But King survived. Four officers were charged with assault and excessive force. Their lawyers argued that the officers believed King was dangerous. They also said the officers were following the police department's policies. The officers were acquitted in a state trial. People rioted for six days in protest. The officers were tried in

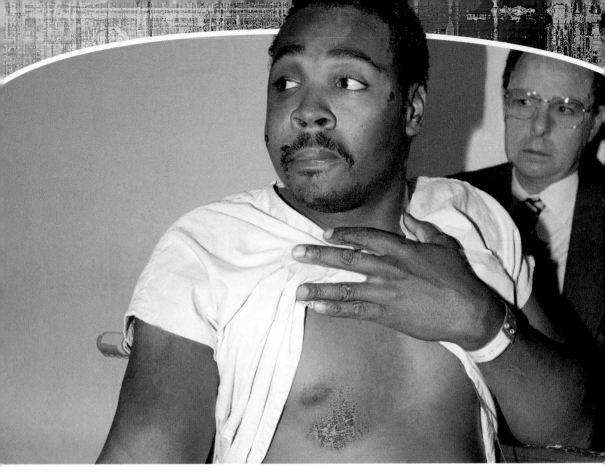

Rodney King shows reporters a bruise on his chest after he was beaten by police officers.

federal court. Two of them were found guilty of violating King's civil rights. They served 30 months in prison.

Nearly 30 years later, another instance of police brutality led to protests and riots. On May 25, 2020, a Black man named George Floyd was reported to police for allegedly using a fake $20 bill. Officers handcuffed Floyd. They forced him to the ground.

Officer Derek Chauvin pressed his knee into Floyd's neck for several minutes. Floyd said he couldn't breathe. Onlookers begged Chauvin to stop. Floyd died. People protested across the country. Protests spread around the world.

Some of the protests became violent. In response, police used more force. They sprayed chemicals that hurt people's eyes, throats, and lungs. They shot rubber bullets. Sometimes police used force on nonviolent protesters.

POLICE BRUTALITY AND HEALTH

Public health issues are health issues that affect a large society. Organizations such as the American Medical Association believe that police brutality is a public health issue. Police brutality causes injuries and deaths.

Police brutality also harms the mental health of people of color. People of color are more likely to experience police brutality, which often leads to fear of police. The fear of police can increase stress. Higher stress can lead to physical health issues. While police brutality is only one factor affecting mental health, researchers say its effects are significant.

BLACK AND BLUE

The Black Lives Matter movement began in 2013. Its organizers want to stop violence against Black communities. They want to affirm the importance of all Black peoples' lives.

A countermovement called Blue Lives Matter sprang up in response. One of its goals is to make attacking a police officer a hate crime. This is a crime motivated by factors such as race or gender. Law professor Frank Rudy Cooper writes, "As a group, [Black people] have been historically subordinated through [slavery], Jim Crow segregation, and ongoing negative stereotypes. Police officers cannot be similarly defined as a historically oppressed minority." Critics of this group note that a person can choose a profession but cannot choose his or her race.

People were angry. This led to more protests.

More people than Floyd and King experienced police brutality. Some were killed by police. Sometimes the officers responsible were fired. But sometimes they were not charged with a crime. In many cases where charges were filed, the officers were acquitted. People often protested in response. They felt that these decisions were unfair.

Very few officers who kill civilians are convicted of a crime. Prosecutors do not charge police officers often. They must meet high standards to prove an officer did something wrong. Laws allow police officers to use force in dangerous situations.

Judges and juries are less likely to convict police officers of a crime than ordinary citizens. Many people have positive opinions of police. They know police officers can feel unsafe on the job. Officers may have little time to make difficult decisions.

FURTHER EVIDENCE

Chapter Three discusses the relationship between race and police brutality, as well as public responses to police brutality. Read the article at the website below. Does the information in the article support the information in the chapter? Does it provide new evidence?

GEORGE FLOYD'S DEATH INSPIRES PROTESTS ALL OVER THE WORLD

abdocorelibrary.com/race-and-policing

THE FUTURE OF AMERICAN POLICING

Inequalities in policing and criminal justice continue today. Many people are advocating for changes. They think the criminal justice system can be made fairer and less violent. But people have different ideas about what changes are needed.

DEFUNDING THE POLICE

One movement is to defund the police. Defunding the police means taking some money away from police departments.

Many people who call for defunding the police also ask for money to be invested in other community services.

The money would be spent on other community programs. People who advocate for this believe police are forced to respond to situations where they are not needed. In many cities, police do not just enforce laws. They also monitor people experiencing homelessness. They respond to people having mental health crises.

Advocates of defunding argue that social workers and others could deal with many of these issues. They could help people with health problems. They could help to reduce or resolve conflicts without violence.

Other city programs could improve situations that lead to crime. These include poverty, lack of housing, and poor education. Money could be taken from police departments and put toward these services instead. Police would only respond to serious crimes and true emergencies.

DISBANDING THE POLICE

Some people want to see the police completely disbanded. Disbanding means there would be no police

Activists who support disbanding want to completely get rid of police forces.

at all, even in the case of violent crimes. However, many people who advocate for disbanding want to replace the police with a different public safety system. Police responsibilities would be moved elsewhere.

Following George Floyd's death in Minneapolis, Minnesota, the Minneapolis City Council began working to disband the city's police department. The council members wanted to build a new community-based department. But there were many obstacles. It would take time to make such a big change.

PERSPECTIVES

THE MINNEAPOLIS POLICE RESPOND

After George Floyd's death, many people demanded change in the Minneapolis Police Department. Some people, including members of the city council, called to defund or disband the police. A group of Minneapolis police officers wrote an open letter. They denounced Derek Chauvin. They said that they wanted to have their opinions heard in the discussion of how policing in Minneapolis would change. They added, "We stand ready to listen and embrace the calls for change, reform and rebuilding. . . . We want to work with you and for you to regain your trust."

Some people in Minneapolis had concerns. People in a majority Black area of Minneapolis voiced their concerns. They saw increases in crime after the city council announced its plans. Some residents sued the city council and mayor. They still wanted reform. But they didn't want to get rid of the police completely.

REFORMING THE POLICE

People in favor of reforming the police don't want to take money from the police. Instead, they want to improve police departments. They argue that better training and certain changes can help prevent police brutality and racism.

Advocates of police reform believe police officers should receive more de-escalation training. This teaches officers how to make situations less dangerous. Many departments do not train officers in de-escalation. Advocates of police reform also want officers to have clear policies. These policies would reduce

RESOURCES BEYOND THE POLICE

Many activists believe that calling the police shouldn't be the first step in some situations. There are situations where police are necessary. But activists point out alternatives to calling the police when people aren't in danger. Examples of these situations include noise complaints, homelessness, and nonviolent crimes. Activists recommend that people use other city and community resources when possible. Some cities have 311 phone lines. People can dial this number to request services, report problems, and ask questions.

discrimination and the use of force. Police could also be required to wear body cameras and follow stricter policies for using them. Many people think it is also important for police to live in the city where they work. This helps them build relationships with the community.

CITIES OF CHANGE

After Floyd's death, many cities decided to make changes. Some agreed to reduce police budgets and spend that money on community programs. Some decided to remove SROs from public schools.

Social worker Erica Rios, *right*, works for the police department in Griffith, Indiana. Some police departments send social workers with police officers to respond to mental health situations.

Some cities already had different programs in place. These programs worked alongside police departments. The CAHOOTS program in Eugene, Oregon, started more than 30 years ago. CAHOOTS stands for Crisis Assistance Helping Out on the Streets. The program's staff are unarmed. They have de-escalation training, crisis training, and knowledge of local resources. They respond to mental health and substance abuse calls. In 2019, CAHOOTS responded to 24,000 calls. The workers only had to call for police backup for 150 of those. The program helps reduce police encounters, which may turn violent. And it helps people get access to resources they need.

Dallas, Texas, uses a program called RIGHT Care. It sends a social worker and health care worker along with police officers responding to mental health situations. Arrests have gone down since the program began.

Other programs work to prevent crime. Some cities partner with outside organizations. Cure Violence works in neighborhoods in New York City, Chicago, and more. It has workers called violence interrupters. Violence interrupters resolve conflicts. Other workers help people at high risk of committing violence. The workers help these people get job training or treatment for drug addiction. In a New York City neighborhood, Cure Violence lowered shootings by 63 percent and gun injuries by 37 percent. Young men in Cure Violence neighborhoods were less supportive of using violence to settle arguments. Less violence was also associated with more confidence in police.

LOOKING FORWARD

The United States has a long history of racist policing. Many racial inequalities continue in policing today. Systemic racism and biased enforcement of policies negatively affect people of color.

People throughout the country have protested police brutality and racist policing. Activists have proposed many changes. Some people have raised concerns about these proposals. But advocates hope that the system can improve and systemic racism can end.

EXPLORE ONLINE

Chapter Four gives an overview of different approaches to changing policing in the United States. Watch the video at the link below. What information does the video provide about ways to reform or reimagine policing? How does that information compare to the information in Chapter Four?

WHAT DOES IT MEAN TO "DEFUND THE POLICE"?

abdocorelibrary.com/race-and-policing

IMPORTANT DATES

1838
The first formal police force in the United States is formed in Boston, Massachusetts. Up until that time, slave patrols policed communities.

1865
The Thirteenth Amendment passes, making slavery illegal but allowing prisons to force people convicted of crimes into unpaid labor.

June 1971
President Richard Nixon declares a War on Drugs. Efforts to reduce drug use and punish people who commit drug crimes increase over the next few decades.

1991
A Black man named Rodney King is beaten by four police officers, causing permanent injuries. The next year, the involved officers are all found not guilty in a state trial. People riot in protest.

2013
The New York City Police Department's stop-and-frisk policy is declared unconstitutional.

October 2015
Officer Ben Fields violently arrests South Carolina student Shakara. He arrests her classmate Niya Kenny for speaking up.

May 25, 2020
In Minneapolis, Minnesota, George Floyd dies after Officer Derek Chauvin kneels on his neck for several minutes. People protest, riot, and demand changes to US policing.

STOP AND THINK

Take a Stand

Many activists believe that schools shouldn't have student resource officers (SROs). SROs may use force against students or unfairly target students of color. But some people believe that they make schools safer. Do you think schools can benefit from having police officers on-site? Or do you think schools can be just as safe without them? Why?

Say What?

Studying racism and the criminal justice system can mean learning a lot of new vocabulary. Find five words in this book you've never heard before. Use a dictionary to find out what they mean. Then write the meanings in your own words and use each word in a new sentence.

Dig Deeper

After reading this book, what questions do you still have about race and policing in the United States? With an adult's help, find a few reliable sources that can help you answer your questions. Write a paragraph about what you learned.

GLOSSARY

acquit
to find not guilty of a crime

advocate
to publicly recommend or argue for something, such as a law or reform

denounce
to publicly criticize something as morally wrong

discriminatory
treating people differently based on something out of their control, such as their race or gender

federal
relating to the national government, rather than state or city governments

prosecutor
a lawyer who charges a person with a crime, often as a representative of the government

rubber bullets
projectiles that are not meant to kill, but can still be dangerous

social worker
a professional who helps people in need and connects them with resources

strike
a time when workers stop working, often to protest something or to get employers to agree to a change

ONLINE RESOURCES

To learn more about race and policing, visit our free resource websites below.

Visit **abdocorelibrary.com** or scan this QR code for free Common Core resources for teachers and students, including vetted activities, multimedia, and booklinks, for deeper subject comprehension.

Visit **abdobooklinks.com** or scan this QR code for free additional online weblinks for further learning. These links are routinely monitored and updated to provide the most current information available.

LEARN MORE

Harris, Duchess. *Black Lives Matter*. Abdo Publishing, 2018.

Harris, Duchess, and Samantha S. Bell. *The Thirteenth Amendment and Its Legacy*. Abdo Publishing, 2020.

ABOUT THE AUTHORS

Duchess Harris, JD, PhD

Dr. Harris is a professor of American Studies and Political Science at Macalester College and curator of the Duchess Harris Collection of ABDO books. She is also the coauthor of the collection, which features popular titles such as *Hidden Human Computers: The Black Women of NASA* and series including Freedom's Promise and Race and American Law. In addition, Dr. Harris hosts the *Freedom's Promise* podcast with her son.

Before working with ABDO, Dr. Harris authored several other books on the topics of race, culture, and American history. She served as an associate editor for *Litigation News*, the American Bar Association Section of Litigation's quarterly flagship publication, and was the first editor in chief of *Law Raza*, an interactive online journal covering race and the law, published at William Mitchell College of Law. She has earned a BA in History from the University of Pennsylvania, a PhD in American Studies from the University of Minnesota, and a JD from William Mitchell College of Law.

R. L. Van

R. L. Van is a writer and editor living in the Twin Cities, Minnesota. She has written nonfiction books on a variety of subjects. In her free time, she enjoys reading, doing crossword puzzles, and caring for her pet cats.

INDEX